Life in the Old West

THE LIFE OF A MINER

Bobbie Kalman & Kate Calder

🍄 Crabtree Publishing Company

LIFE IN THE OLD WEST

Created by Bobbie Kalman

To Eileen McNab, a cherished gem

Editor-in-Chief
Bobbie Kalman

Writing team
Bobbie Kalman
Kate Calder

Researcher
Amelinda Berube

Managing editor
Lynda Hale

Editors
Niki Walker
Jane Lewis

Copy editors
Heather Levigne
Hannelore Sotzek

Computer design
Lynda Hale
Campbell Creative Services (cover)

Consultant
Chic Di Francia, Comstock History Store; Virginia City, Nevada

Special thanks to
Donna Jones, The Empire Mine; Boyd Nichol, Bisbee Museum and Historical Society; Debra Neiswonger, Colorado Historical Society; Kathryn Totton, University of Nevada; William A. Hastings, Littleton Historical Museum; Mary Helmich, California State Parks; Sutter's Fort, Sacramento; Carol Clifford; Jim Bowman, Glenbow Archives, Calgary

Photographs and reproductions
Noella Ballenger: page 16; The Bancroft Library, University of California, Berkeley: pages 20 (top), 21 (top left); Bisbee Mining and Historical Museum: pages 13 (top), 15, 20 (bottom), 21 (top right, bottom), 27; California State Parks: pages 12, 20 (top); Colorado Historical Society: title page (F-12030A), pages 22 (F-16321), 23 (F-43013), 24 (F-43015), 25 (F-44349); Denver Public Library: page 27 (bottom); Eyewire, Inc.: page 4; courtesy of the Littleton Historical Museum: page 25 (bottom); National Museum of American Art, Washington DC/Art Resource, NY: pages 30-31 (detail); Tony and Alba Sanches-Zinnanti: page 13 (bottom); Seaver Center for Western History Research, Los Angeles County Museum of Natural History: pages 6-7; Special Collections, University of Nevada-Reno Library: pages 14 (top), 26

Illustrations and colorizations
Barbara Bedell: cover, pages 5, 10, 11, 12, 14, 15, 17, 18, 19, 23, 25
Bonna Rouse: pages 8-9, 16-17, 28-29, 30

Crabtree Publishing Company

PMB 16A	360 York Road,	73 Lime Walk
350 Fifth Avenue,	RR 4	Headington,
Suite 3308	Niagara-on-the-Lake,	Oxford
New York, NY	Ontario, Canada	OX3 7AD
10118	L0S 1J0	United Kingdom

Cataloging in Publication Data
Kalman, Bobbie
The life of a miner
(Life in the Old West)
Includes index.
ISBN 0-7787-0077-1 (library bound) ISBN 0-7787-0109-3 (pbk.)
This book describes the hard rock mining industry that developed in the North American west following the gold rush, including the operations of a mine and the lives of the miners and their families.
1. Gold miners—West (U.S.)—History—Juvenile literature. 2. Gold miners—Canada, Western—History—Juvenile literature. 3. Gold mines and mining—West (U.S.)—History—Juvenile literature. 4. Gold mines and mining—Canada, Western—History—Juvenile literature. [1. Gold mines and mining—West (North America)—History.] I. Calder, Kate. II. Title. III. Series: Kalman, Bobbie. Life in the Old West.
HD 8039.M732U653 1999   j622'.3422'0978   LC 99-23488
CIP

TABLE OF CONTENTS

THE BIRTH OF AN INDUSTRY

In the early 1800s, the North American West was inhabited mostly by Native North Americans whose **ancestors** had lived there for generations. Most of the people who had come from Europe lived in the eastern states and provinces. Few made the long and difficult journey across plains and over mountains to reach the western frontier. For years, the West was mostly unsettled.

In 1848, gold was discovered in California. News of the discovery spread quickly across the continent and around the world. By 1849, people from all over the world were headed to California with hopes of striking it rich. They traveled across seas in ships and crossed hundreds of miles of land in **covered wagons**. This huge westward movement was known as the **California gold rush**.

New arrivals

The people who went to California in search of gold were known as **prospectors**. Prospectors, who were usually men, looked for an area of unsettled land and claimed it as their own. Few women made the difficult journey to the western frontier.

Staking a claim

The first order of business for prospectors was to **stake a claim**, or mark an area to call their own. They set up tents or built shacks along riverbanks and marked the claim with signs, wooden pegs, or tools. Prospectors usually worked together in small groups.

Registering claims

Prospectors registered their claims at the **commissioner's office**. Registering a claim meant that the prospector was the legal owner of the property. Owning a claim prevented others from stealing it and allowed the owner to sell it as he or she wished.

Finding gold

Prospectors found gold in many forms—dust, small flakes, or nuggets. Gold was scattered along riverbeds or buried just below the surface of the ground. These sources of gold bits were called **placer deposits**. **Placer gold** was often found in the bends of rivers and streams, where the current of the water was slower, and gold settled to the bottom over time.

(opposite page) When prospectors first arrived in California, they often crouched for hours hoping to find flecks of gold in their pans.

Panning for gold was the earliest and simplest form of mining. Prospectors looked for gold in placer deposits by swishing dirt and gravel in a shallow pan of water. When they poured out the water, the gravel went with it. The gold bits were heavier, so they stayed in the pan.

*To wash large amounts of gravel, prospectors used large wooden boxes called **cradles**, which they rocked back and forth.*

*A long trough called a **sluice** was also used to wash the gold. Its **riffled**, or ridged, bottom caught the gold as water ran over large amounts of gravel.*

HARD-ROCK MINING

After gold was found in California, it was also discovered in Nevada, Colorado, British Columbia, the Yukon, and Alaska. Each discovery brought a rush of prospectors to the West. As more people found gold, placer deposits began to disappear. The only gold that remained was buried deep below the ground's surface in large deposits called **lodes**. Lodes were also known as **vein deposits** because they lay in long, branching lines that resembled veins in the underground rock. Rock containing precious metals such as gold or silver is known as **ore**.

Harder to find

People searched for lodes of gold in areas where placer gold was found. Lodes of gold were much more difficult to mine than placer deposits because they were deep underground. Deep **shafts**, or downward passageways, were **excavated**, or dug into the earth. This method of mining was called **hard-rock mining**. Prospectors tried creating shafts. In most cases, however, the rock was too hard to dig through, and the miners did not have the proper equipment to locate the lodes of gold.

Hard-rock mining

Teams of men and machinery were needed to reach a lode and then separate it from the rock. Companies that could afford to buy the machinery and hire workers began establishing mines. Although the mines were set up to find large lodes of gold, other valuable minerals such as silver and copper were also found.

Mining helps the West

Mining was an important industry in the development of the West. In the last half of the 1800s, hundreds of hard-rock mines were established. Many people were attracted to the West because of the mining jobs that were available. Companies often established towns and communities, and many people became wealthy.

INSIDE A MINE

A mine was a series of underground tunnels, shafts, and rooms called **chambers**. To create the mine, a deep shaft was dug in the earth beside an area where there was a lode. At the bottom of the shaft, a tunnel was dug across to where the lode was located. Miners began constructing the mine upwards along the lode. They extracted ore from the lode in areas called **stopes**.

Old stopes, new stopes

As the mine grew and new stopes were formed, old stopes were filled with leftover rock to keep the mine from caving in. The miners carted rock through tunnels to the main shaft where it was hauled to the surface. Hundreds of miners worked underground all day, continually drilling, blasting, shoveling, and sending rock to the surface.

stope

*Hot underground water seeped into the tunnels. It was collected in a pit called the **sump** at the bottom of the mine shaft. From the sump, the water was pumped up to the surface to keep the mine as dry as possible.*

*The miners and equipment were brought up and down the **main shaft** in elevator cages.*

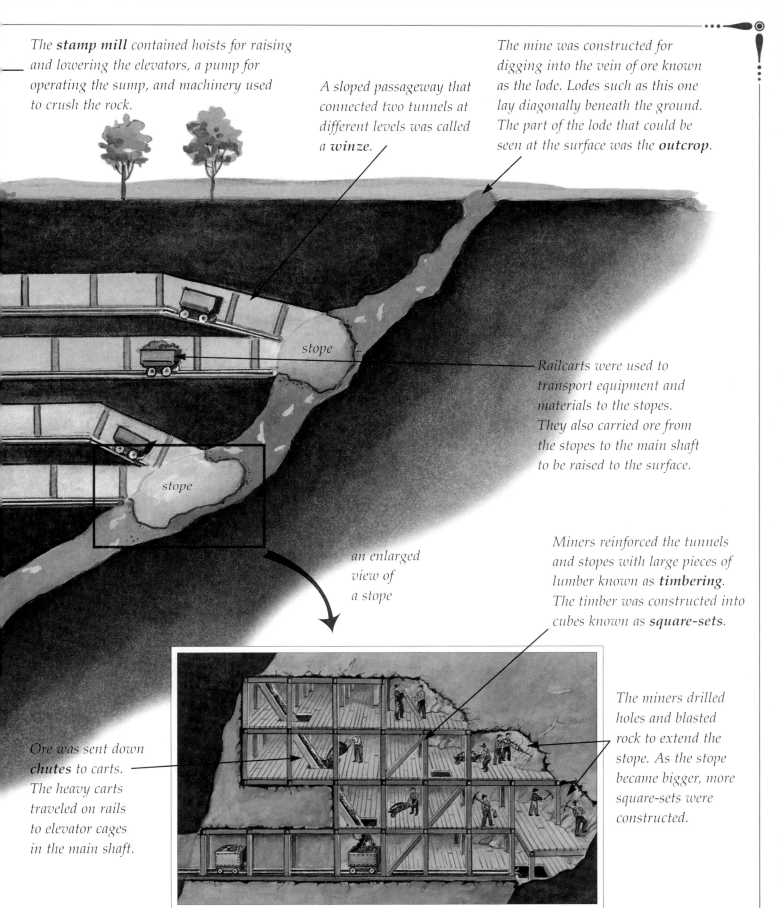

The **stamp mill** contained hoists for raising and lowering the elevators, a pump for operating the sump, and machinery used to crush the rock.

A sloped passageway that connected two tunnels at different levels was called a **winze**.

The mine was constructed for digging into the vein of ore known as the lode. Lodes such as this one lay diagonally beneath the ground. The part of the lode that could be seen at the surface was the **outcrop**.

stope

stope

Railcarts were used to transport equipment and materials to the stopes. They also carried ore from the stopes to the main shaft to be raised to the surface.

an enlarged view of a stope

Miners reinforced the tunnels and stopes with large pieces of lumber known as **timbering**. The timber was constructed into cubes known as **square-sets**.

The miners drilled holes and blasted rock to extend the stope. As the stope became bigger, more square-sets were constructed.

Ore was sent down **chutes** to carts. The heavy carts traveled on rails to elevator cages in the main shaft.

When miners were finished working in a square-set, they filled it in with extra rock to prevent a cave-in.

A MINER'S TOOLS

Breaking and lifting heavy rock all day required reliable equipment. Miners used a variety of strong, sturdy tools to help them loosen and crush chunks of rock. They also used explosives to blast away large amounts of hard rock to extend the tunnels through the mine.

(left) A sharp pickax was used to break rock away from tunnel walls.

(right) A shovel was used to load ore into carts.

Lanterns were the brightest source of light underground. This simple lantern used only a candle. Others were fueled with oil and could burn for longer periods of time.

Miners wore a hat made of stiffened cloth to protect their head from falling rubble. The cloth was coated with layers of glue until it was almost as sturdy as a modern hardhat. A candleholder was fitted around the hat. The holder allowed the miner to keep both hands free for working.

Miners often attached candles to the wall with a candleholder. Each miner kept two or three extra candles and some matches in a waterproof container to provide light for his entire shift.

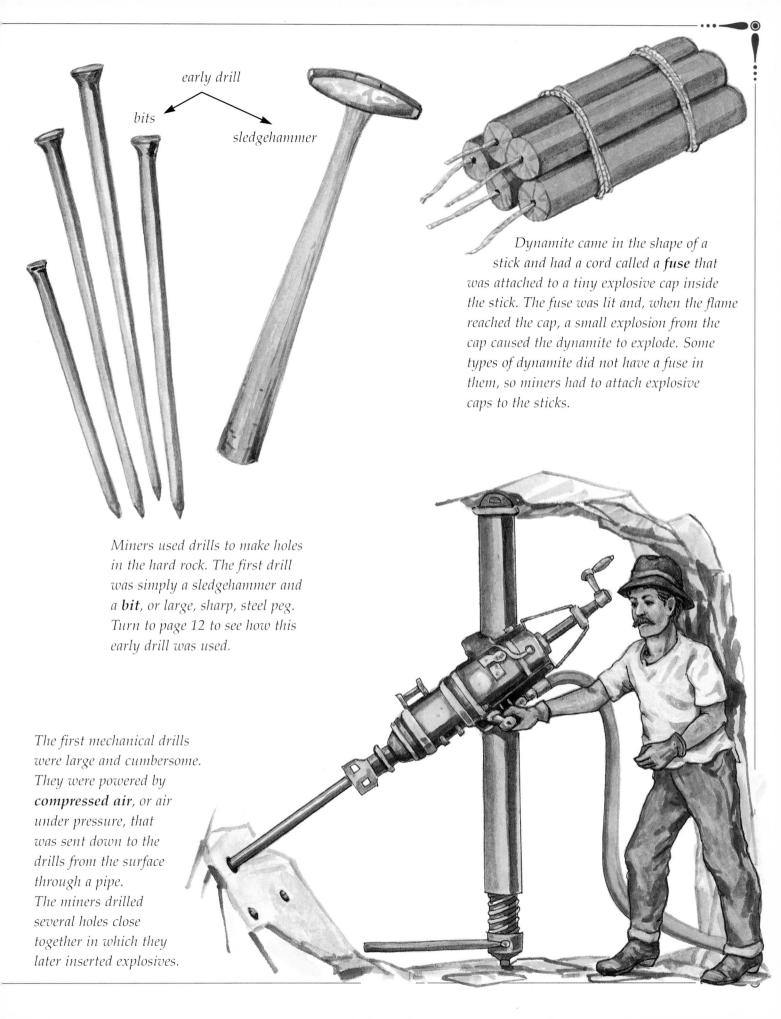

early drill

bits

sledgehammer

Dynamite came in the shape of a stick and had a cord called a **fuse** that was attached to a tiny explosive cap inside the stick. The fuse was lit and, when the flame reached the cap, a small explosion from the cap caused the dynamite to explode. Some types of dynamite did not have a fuse in them, so miners had to attach explosive caps to the sticks.

Miners used drills to make holes in the hard rock. The first drill was simply a sledgehammer and a **bit**, or large, sharp, steel peg. Turn to page 12 to see how this early drill was used.

The first mechanical drills were large and cumbersome. They were powered by **compressed air**, or air under pressure, that was sent down to the drills from the surface through a pipe. The miners drilled several holes close together in which they later inserted explosives.

At Work in the Mines

Double-jacking was dangerous—a miner could miss the top of the drill bit and hurt the other miner's hand!

Every morning, miners lined up to ride in elevators or cages down into the mine. Once underground, they split into small groups. Each group was assigned work in a different area of the mine.

Drillers

In some mines, workers swung heavy picks all day, loosening rock from the walls or breaking large pieces of rock into smaller pieces. In many mines, the rock was too hard to break from the walls with a pick. The miners made holes in the rock by **single-jacking**, or hammering a long drill bit into the rock with a sledgehammer. Sometimes drilling was shared by two men, which was known as **double-jacking**. Once holes were made, miners stuffed them with explosives, and the rock was blown apart.

The shafts were often tight spaces, so being short was an advantage in this job—tall miners had to crouch or kneel in the tunnels. It was difficult to spend a whole day in that position. This miner is drilling a steel bit into the rock.

Rock movers

Miners known as **muckers** shoveled piles of rock into railcarts to be taken to the surface. The carts were hauled away by mules or rolled along the tracks. Every day, muckers had a **quota**, or minimum number, of carts to fill with broken ore. Muckers also laid rail tracks and built square-sets.

"Fire in the hole!"

In the early days of mining, miners known as **blasters** made explosives by filling paper tubes with explosive **black powder** and inserting a fuse. The blaster then put a tube into a hole in the rock and lit the fuse. He yelled, "Fire in the hole!" to warn other miners of the coming explosion and ran as fast as he could from the burning fuse. Each explosion extended the tunnel by three feet after the rubble was shoveled away.

Bigger blasts, better drills

Eventually, new technology was developed to cut faster and deeper into the rock. Black powder was replaced by dynamite, which could blast away much more rock with each explosion. Blasting was done at the end of a shift because explosions filled the mines with dust and dirt.

The end of a hard day

At the end of the day, miners were transported slowly up to ground level from the sweltering mines. To prevent illness, they changed out of their filthy, sweat-soaked clothing before going up to the cool outside air. Some companies required miners to change their clothes before leaving to prevent them from smuggling ore in their pockets, boots, or cuffs. Stealing ore was called **high-grading**.

The machine drill in this picture was large and heavy. It took three men to operate, but it made drilling holes a much quicker and easier process.

Each railcart could hold one ton of ore. A mucker shoveled up to 20 carts of ore in one day. These railcarts were pulled by a small locomotive.

Lunch pails were ideal for heating water for tea or coffee. Miners held the pail over a candle that was placed in the middle of a circle of nails hammered into a wooden plank.

(top) The miners became so hot working in the mines that many worked shirtless to stay cool.

Some miners went to work before sunrise and had only a few short breaks during the day. After their shift, there was little spare time before going to bed. Other miners worked their shift at night. They arrived home before sunrise and slept during the day. Many miners saw daylight only on Sunday—their one day off a week.

Feeling the heat

Working in the mines could be extremely hot. Miners naturally worked up a sweat as they swung picks and shoveled rubble, but sometimes the miners uncovered **thermal springs** while digging. These springs of hot water caused the temperature inside the tunnel to be almost unbearable.

Dining underground

Miners carried their lunch in a tin pail and stored it in the underground lunch room. The pails were placed on shelves or hung near the ceiling to make it difficult for rats to get the food. At some mines, the workers had to send their pails to the surface after lunch. The mine owners did not want the miners to use their pails to steal ore.

Good luck and bad luck

Many miners were **superstitious**—they believed in signs of both good and bad luck. Some men carried horseshoes and other charms into the mines, hoping these objects would bring good luck. They nailed the horseshoes onto timbers where they worked. Crows were considered bad luck. If a crow flew over a miner's head as he walked to work, he would return home. If a miner dreamed of an accident or disaster, he often avoided mining that day.

Ghosts

It was easy to be scared by the darkness and stillness of the tunnels as well as the spooky sounds that echoed down empty shafts. Many miners were afraid that there were ghosts in the mines. They believed that a ghost was the spirit of a miner killed on the job and whose body was never recovered.

Practical jokes

Miners often played practical jokes on new workers. They asked newcomers to complete an impossible task such as filling a barrel with smoke. A common prank was nailing a lunch pail to the shelf. When a miner unsuccessfully tried to pick it up, everyone laughed. Coats were often nailed to the wall where they hung. Some tricksters scared new miners by pretending to be ghosts. A few miners were so terrified by the tricks that they quit!

*Horses and mules were lowered by large **pulleys** into a mine to help pull heavy carts filled with rock. Often a horse or mule spent the rest of its life underground. In later years, small locomotives were used to pull carts.*

THE STAMP MILL

Once the ore arrived at the surface, it was crushed until it was as fine as sand. This process took place in a large building called a stamp mill. Most large mines had their own stamp mill. Some mines, however, sent their ore to a stamp mill owned and operated by another company. Rock was crushed in the stamp mill, and the gold, silver, or copper was then ready to be **refined**, or separated from the ore with chemicals. Some stamp mills had the equipment needed to refine precious metals in the same building. Others had a separate building called the refinery where the rock was sent after it was crushed in the stamp mill.

Follow the numbers to learn how gold was separated from ore at the stamp mill.

*A small building attached to the stamp mill contained coal-burning **boilers**, which produced steam to power the stamp mill.*

6. *The mixture of rock and chemicals was then put into **steam-heated pans** where the pure gold, silver, or copper was separated from the ore.*

The gray building is an old stamp mill at an abandoned mine in Bodie, California. Point to where the ore was brought into the stamp mill.

1. Ore from the mine was brought into the stamp mill in carts.

2. The ore went through crushing machines that broke it into small chunks.

3. **Stamps** broke the ore into even smaller pieces.

4. In some stamp mills, the ore was put onto **vanners**, which were wide, rotating belts that helped separate the precious metal from the rock.

5. **Amalgamating pans** combined the ore with chemicals and melted it into a paste.

7. When the gold was separated from the ore, it was poured into molds. It cooled and hardened into bars.

Hazards

Working in a mine was a dangerous job. In some large mines, a worker was killed almost every week. Some miners died by falling down the long shafts. Many fell to their death on the way to the surface. After being in the hot mine all day, the cool air near the top caused miners to faint and fall backward down the steep shaft. Others fell into the sump and were badly burned or killed. Sometimes people were injured or killed by rocks or tools that accidentally were dropped down a shaft.

When tunnels **caved in**, or collapsed, falling rock and timber crushed miners or trapped them in a small space where they quickly ran out of air to breathe. Fortunately, miners had ways of telling when a cave-in was about to happen. If rats suddenly scurried about, the miners knew they had to hurry out of the tunnels. Sometimes the timbers in a mine would creak and groan for days before a collapse. Experienced miners could tell how close the cave-in was by these sounds.

(above) The timbering in the mines often was not strong enough to support the weight of the rock above and prevent a cave-in. (opposite page) These miners have been caught by a blast that went off accidentally.

Dusty air

Hard-rock miners suffered from a unique illness called **miner's consumption**, which was caused by the rock dust that filled the air in mines. When miners breathed in the air, the heavy dust filled their lungs. They developed a harsh, hacking cough that often lead to death. Dynamite blasting also created harmful dust and fumes in the air. Miners choked on the dusty air. Some collapsed if they breathed the air right after a dynamite blast.

Fire

Since candles and oil lanterns were the only source of light, fire was always a threat in the mines. To prevent fires, miners kept their candles away from the timbers that supported the mine shaft. Many mines had only one shaft leading to the surface. If a fire blocked the shaft, the miners had no way of escaping.

Dynamite

Dynamite was used to blast ore from the mine. It exploded easily, so miners handled it carefully. When a stick of dynamite was set to go off, the men hid. If it did not explode, they came out. Sometimes the blast went off just as the miners returned, killing them. If the dynamite did not explode, it was removed from the rock so that other miners would not unknowingly drill into it and set off an explosion. The caps used to ignite explosives were also dangerous. Miners often lost fingers when they handled them.

One for all and all for one

When there was an accident or a cave-in, no one hesitated to join a rescue party, even if the rescue was dangerous. Men stopped what they were doing and went to help. When a miner was killed on the job, the whole company of miners usually stopped working for the day.

Some hard-rock miners grew up in a mining community. Some were prospectors who had not found gold and needed to find a job. Others were criminals who were trying to hide from the law or make a new start in life.

From all over

The mines attracted men from North America, Europe, England, Germany, Mexico, China, and Australia. In spite of their different backgrounds, miners had two important things in common: they spent long and difficult days in the mines, and they were all proud to be miners.

(above) Miners at the Empire Mine in California squeezed into long **skips**, or railcars, that took them down into the mine tunnels.

(left) The workers inside this copper mine stamp mill are taking a break from operating the huge machinery that separates copper from the rock.

(top left) Many miners came from Cornwall, England. They had years of experience working in the tin mines in Cornwall. Cornish men **immigrated** to North America to find work in the gold mines. They shared their mining knowledge and often became supervisors.

(above and left) Miners went to a photography studio to have their portraits taken. They sent the portraits to their families. The men in the picture on the left posed with their lunch pails and candles.

Homes in the Old West were often plain and simple. They did not have running water or electricity. The homes of most miners were cramped, cold, dirty, and uncomfortable. The dirty conditions attracted mice, lice, and bedbugs.

Renting

Unmarried miners often rented a room in a hotel for a short period of time when they were looking for work in a new mining town. **Boarding houses** were large homes that rented rooms and provided three meals a day to miners at a far cheaper rate than hotels. Some miners with room to spare rented out cots in their home.

Quick and temporary

Miners did not have the time to build solid, comfortable houses, and ready-made homes were too expensive. Most miners built temporary homes that were little more than rough shacks. They spent most of their time at the mine and rarely improved their home. If the mine went out of business, they left their home behind and moved to a different town to find work.

There was little room for more than a bed, table, and a few chairs in this miner's shack. He could only entertain one visitor at a time.

Company housing

Some mining companies built houses in the town near the mine. They rented these homes to their workers. Many miners lived in a company **dormitory** or **dorm**. A dorm is a large building that provides places to sleep for many people. A company dorm housed 20 or 30 men. It was a simple building located close to the mine. Miners who had houses some distance from the mines stayed at the dorm throughout the week and went home to their family on Sundays. Other miners stayed at the dorm every night.

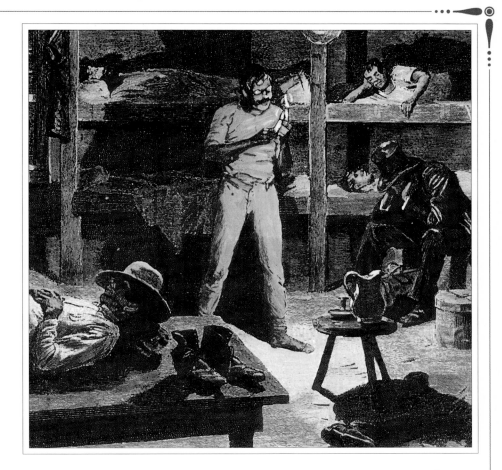

(top) These miners sleep in a dorm at night. Which one has just arrived from the city to work in the mine?
(bottom) This mining family built a small shack using wooden planks.

Most miners working in the early mines were single men. There were few women living in the West in the mid-1800s. In later years, the West became populated with both men and women, filling the mining communities with families.

Many jobs for women

Women worked hard to keep the household running while their husband was working in the mine. They did all the cleaning, cooking, washing, mending, and child-raising. Being married to a miner was stressful for a woman. If her husband became sick, injured, or was killed, she would have to work to support the family as well as run a home.

A kid's life

Children helped with household chores such as feeding chickens and weeding the garden. Older children looked after their younger sisters and brothers. Some were able to earn money for the family by delivering newspapers or helping a tradesperson such as the blacksmith.

Children underground

Boys who worked underground had to be at least ten years old. Some worked at the mine as **tool nippers**. Tool nippers went through the tunnels and picked up broken tools so they could be repaired at the blacksmith shop. They also lit candles under the miners' lunch pails so the food would be warm by lunchtime.

One-room schools

Schools had only one classroom and one teacher for all grades. Children learned mathematics, reading, writing, geography, and history. Most children in mining towns, however, spent little time in school. Many parents did not think that an education was important and kept their children at home to do chores instead. They expected their boys to become miners and girls to be housewives when they grew up.

Warning whistles

Whenever an accident happened at the mine, a loud steam whistle was blown. Whistles from other mines and mills in the area would join in, quickly filling the entire town with their shrill sound. Family members panicked whenever they heard the whistle for fear that it was their husband, father, son, or brother who had been injured or killed.

(top) These children are riding on a mule that pulled ore to the stamp mill. Is there room for one more? (bottom) This woman is putting peas on a string to dry them. Most women worked at home taking care of their household. Some taught in schools or worked in stores.

THE COMPANY STORE

In many mining towns there was only one store where miners and their families could buy supplies. The store was owned by the mining company. The company store carried everything the community needed—items such as clothing, groceries, luggage, carpet, fabric, medicine, lumber, and buggies. The miners and other townspeople did all their shopping at this store.

Credit

Some mining companies paid the miners with store coupons rather than with money. Other company stores gave the miners **credit**, which meant they could take things without paying for them right away. The company then took the money out of the miners' paychecks.

The miners had no choice but to buy what they needed at the company store. Many miners owed the store so much money that they were in debt for the rest of their lives.

The company town

Some mining companies owned not only the store but also the bank and all the property around the mine. The bank gave a miner a loan to build a house and then took money from the miner's paycheck to repay the loan. The mining company also allowed the miner to build his house on property near the mine. The company, however, still owned the property. It could force the miner and his family out of their home at any time if a company decided to use that land for expanding the mine.

The company store was a gathering place where people met with friends while they shopped. Since it was usually the only place to get food and equipment, store owners often charged far more than the goods were worth.

WORKERS' RIGHTS

Miners worked in dangerous, difficult, and unhealthy conditions. To keep costs low, some companies did not provide safe working conditions for the miners. The miners were seldom paid fair wages for their work. Rent, food, and supplies became more expensive over time, but the wages rarely increased.

Forming labor unions

Large mining companies often ignored workers' complaints about their conditions and wages. To get the company to pay attention, miners formed **unions**. These organizations gave the miners a strong, unified voice for expressing their concerns. Most company owners disapproved of unions and did their best to prevent them from forming.

Out of work

If a union's demands were ignored, the workers organized a **strike**. During a strike, all the miners stopped working and refused to begin again until the company improved their working conditions. Some strikes lasted for months before the union's demands were met. Everyone was unhappy during a strike. Neither the company nor the miners made any money.

Anyone who dared to work during a strike had to cross the **picket line** and face the anger of fellow miners. Everyone wanted to resolve the problem as soon as possible. Meetings between the union leaders and the company usually ended in a **compromise**, in which each side gave up some of its demands.

Unions held large picnics for the miners and their families. One of the activities at a picnic was a drilling contest. Miners competed in pairs on a platform stage to see which pair was the fastest at double-jacking a hole.

Boomtowns

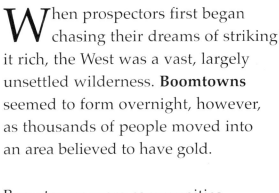

W hen prospectors first began chasing their dreams of striking it rich, the West was a vast, largely unsettled wilderness. **Boomtowns** seemed to form overnight, however, as thousands of people moved into an area believed to have gold.

Boomtowns were communities that grew quickly. The ones that began as a result of placer-gold deposits often grew and became more established after hard-rock mining companies moved in.

Businesses bloomed

Businesses were established quickly wherever a community formed. Merchants and tradespeople sold goods and services to the prospectors and miners. Several businesses started because the mining company needed their goods or services.

Blacksmiths repaired drill bits, and machinists made machines used to separate the metal from the ore. Look at the businesses on these two pages and write a sentence about how each one was important to the people in a mining town.

The lumber industry

Mines needed lumber for the timber supports in the tunnels. To create timber for some large mines, entire forests were cut down. The wood used for timbering for the mines in Virginia City (see page 29) was enough to build over 25,000 houses. Lumber was also used to build the stamp mill and all the stores and houses in a boomtown.

The saloon

Miners, merchants, and other workers often spent their free time at the saloon. There they met with friends to play card games and talk.

Ghost towns

Some towns became **ghost towns** as quickly as they became boomtowns. After all the minerals were extracted, the mining company closed the mine. The miners moved to other towns to find new jobs. Without the miners and their families, there were not enough people to buy goods or services from the businesses in town. Businesses shut down, and more people moved away. Eventually, empty buildings and roads were all that were left.

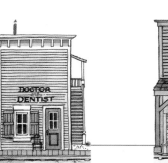

Famous Mines of the West

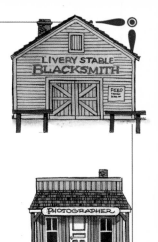

Hundreds of mines were built across western North America in the mid- to late 1800s. Many of them lasted only a few years, until the minerals were **depleted**, or removed.

They were then shut down. Some mines, however, lasted for decades and are still operating today. They grew bigger over the years and have employed thousands of miners.

The **Cameron Mine** was one of the most profitable gold mines in the **Cariboo** region of British Columbia. This was the most successful region for gold mining in British Columbia. The **Kootenay** region in Southern British Columbia also had many profitable mines.

The **Anaconda Mine** in Butte, Montana, was the world's biggest copper mine by the end of the 1800s. As more communities acquired electricity, copper wires and cables were needed to operate electrical devices and telephone wires.

The **Empire Mine** in California was one of the first hard-rock gold mines in North America.

The **Homestake Mine**, located in the Black Hills in Lead, South Dakota, was the largest gold-mining operation in North America.

The **Comstock Lode** was the biggest lode of silver in North America during the late 1870s. It was located in Virginia City, Nevada. New mining techniques were developed in the Comstock mines.

The **Copper Queen Mine** made Bisbee, Arizona one of the largest mining towns in North America in the 1800s. It produced large amounts of copper, as well as gold and silver.

NATIVE LAND

Before European settlers arrived in the West, the land on which mines were established was home to Native Americans. For centuries, these **aboriginal**, or native, peoples hunted wild animals, fished, and grew crops to feed their families. Many groups of Native Americans moved from place to place in search of animals to hunt. They hunted buffalo, which provided them with food and skins to make clothing and shelter. Their way of life was destroyed by the settlers and miners.

When gold was discovered in the 1800s, thousands of prospectors moved onto lands where Native Americans lived. Settlers dammed and polluted rivers to build mines, killing fish and wild animals that the aboriginal people needed for food. Settlers hunted thousands of buffalo for their hide or just for sport. They also brought diseases that caused thousands of Native Americans to die. The aboriginal people began to resent the settlers and miners.

Reservations

With fewer animals to hunt, the aboriginal people began stealing livestock and fighting with the miners over land. The government made **treaties**, or agreements, with the Native Americans, which allowed them to live on certain areas of land called **reservations**. These lands were not fertile enough for growing crops, and there were few wild animals to hunt. The government promised to give the Native Americans food and materials for making clothing and homes. These supplies, however, were not nearly enough to feed and support the aboriginal families.

Battles over land

As more gold was discovered in the West, miners began moving onto land that had been given to Native Americans. At first the government tried to stop the miners from going onto the Native territories, but the mines were too profitable and provided hundreds of jobs. The miners would not leave. The government asked the Native people if they would sell the lands to the government. When they refused, the army was sent to force them off the land. Many people were killed in violent battles, such as the ones that took place in the Black Hills of South Dakota.

GLOSSARY

ancestor A person from whom another person is descended

black powder An explosive substance used for blasting rock in early mining days

boarding house A place that provides meals and a place to sleep in exchange for pay

commissioner's office The office at which prospectors paid for and registered their claims so others could not claim the same land

compromise A solution to an argument in which both sides work together and give up some of their demands

covered wagon A wagon with a canvas top

credit An arrangement in which something that has been purchased can be paid for at a later time

fuse A piece of string that burns at a steady rate and is used to light explosives

immigrate To come to live in another country permanently

panning The process of using a pan and water to separate gold from gravel

picket line A group of workers carrying signs, blocking the entrance to a workplace, and refusing to work in protest of working conditions (see strike)

placer gold Deposits of gold found in riverbeds and shallow underground areas

strike A situation in which workers refuse to work until their demands for better working conditions or an increase in pay are met

thermal spring A natural flow of hot water coming from within the earth

union A group of workers that forms an organization whose object is to ensure fair working conditions and higher pay

INDEX

1 2 3 4 5 6 7 8 9 0   Printed in the U.S.A.   8 7 6 5 4 3 2 1 0 9